Helping Children See Jesus

ISBN: 978-1-933206-28-8

God's Faithfulness
Old Testament Volume 15
Deuteronomy

Author: Doris Stuber Moose
Illustrator: Vernon Henkel
Page Layout: Morgan Melton, Patricia Pope

© Bible Visuals International
PO Box 153, Akron, PA 17501-0153
Phone: (717) 859-1131
www.biblevisuals.org

All rights reserved. No part of this publication may be reproduced, stored in a retrieval system or transmitted in any form by any means, electronic, mechanical, photocopy, recording or otherwise, without the prior permission of the publisher, except as provided by USA copyright law.

RELATED ITEMS

To access related items (such as activities, memory verse posters and translated texts) please visit our web store at www.biblevisuals.org and enter 2015 at the top right of the web page. You may need to reduce the zoom setting to get the search box.

FREE TEXT DOWNLOAD

To obtain a FREE printable copy of the English teaching text (PDF format) under Product Format, please scroll down and select Extra–PDF Teacher Text Download. Then under Language select English before clicking the ADD TO CART button to place in your shopping cart. Other languages are available at an additional cost from the Language menu. When checking out, use coupon code XTACSV17 at checkout and click on Apply Coupon to receive the discount on the English text.

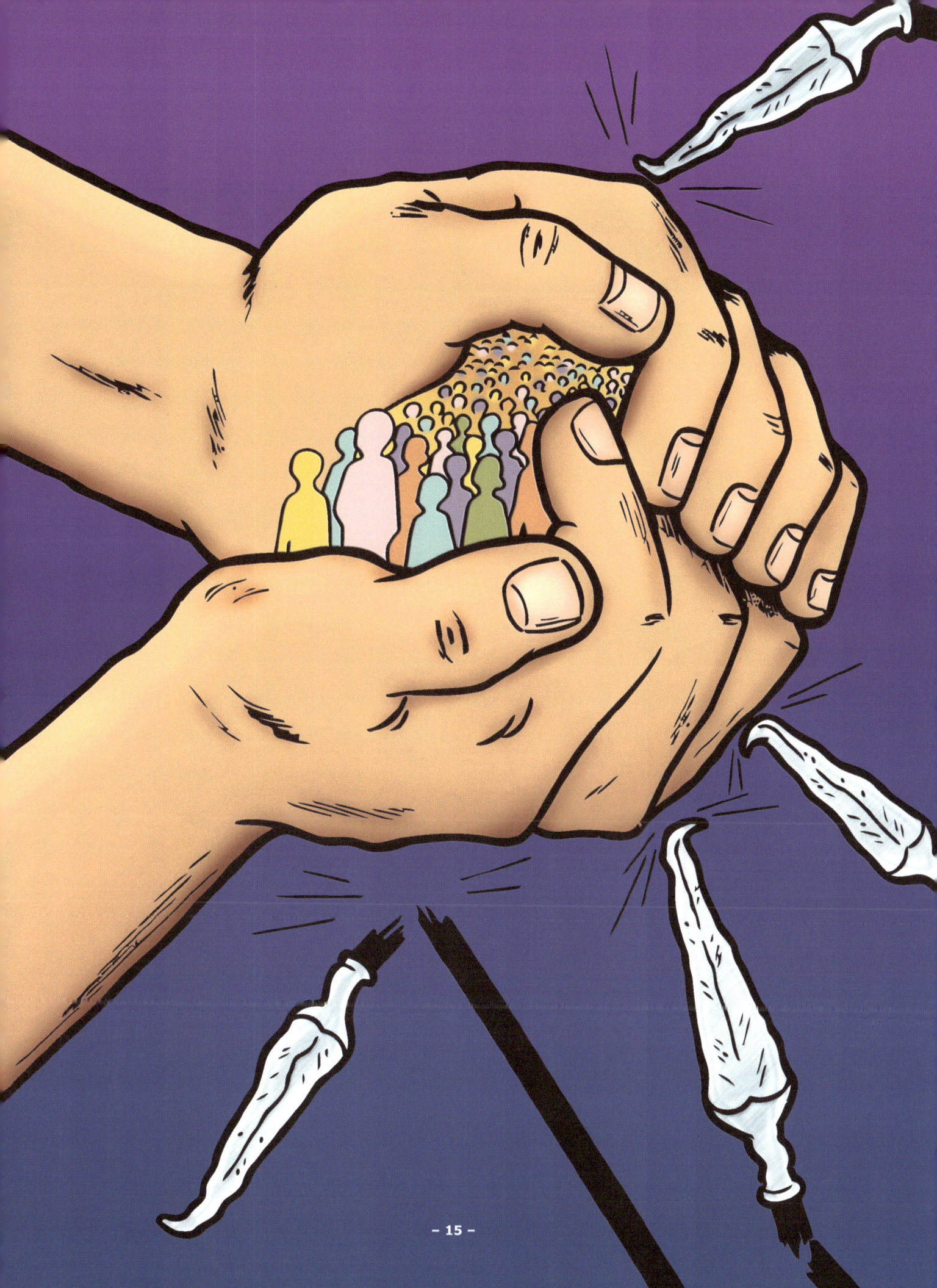

The LORD thy God, He is God, the faithful God.

Deuteronomy 7:9a

© Bible Visuals International Inc

Lesson 1
LESSONS IN OBEDIENCE

NOTE TO THE TEACHER

Deuteronomy is the last of the five books God gave through Moses. Its teaching prepared the Israelite people for living in Canaan. Deuteronomy has been called *The Book of Review* or *The Book of Remembrance* because it rehearses: (1) the past history of the people of Israel (chapters 1-4) and (2) God's Law which He had given to the Israelites (chapters 5-26). In addition, Deuteronomy reveals the future of Israel (chapters 27-28). And it includes important teaching for God's people today. (See 1 Corinthians 10:11.)

Over and over, Moses pleads with the people to "hear" the Word of God, "keep" it, and "do" it. Only by knowing God's Word and obeying it could they live successfully in the land which He had promised them. He wanted them to obey because of their love for Him.

Moses gave these instructions and warnings shortly before his death at age 120. People lived longer in those days. So Moses was still strong, vigorous and had good eyesight. (See Deuteronomy 34:7.) Those who were 20 years old or older when they left Egypt (except Joshua and Caleb) had died in the wilderness for murmuring against God. (See Numbers 14:29.) The younger people needed to be prepared for life in their new land. So they were commanded to "remember" what had happened earlier. (See Deuteronomy 1:1—4:43; 5:15; 6:12; 8:2, 11, 18; 9:7, 24:9; 25:17.) Remembering the faithfulness of God should cause them to love and obey Him. However they needed to be warned that they would be disciplined for disobedience as were their fathers.

In the last lesson of the preceding volume (*Death: The Wages of Sin*, Volume 14), we learned that even the great leader Moses was punished for disobedience. God would not allow him to enter the wonderful land of Canaan. Disobeying the Lord God is serious business! The teachings of the book of Deuteronomy, therefore, demand earnest attention.

As you recall, we closed the last lesson with the account of Moses' death. Our study of Deuteronomy, however, covers the events of the last events of Moses' life. Make this clear to your students.

Scripture to be studied: Deuteronomy 1:1-4:43

The *aim* of the lesson: To show that God, who is faithful, blesses those who obey Him.

What your students should *know*: God's correction of His children shows His love for them.

What your students should *feel*: Eager to obey God and honor Him.

What your students should *do*: Determine how they will obey God and honor Him during the coming week.

Lesson outline (for the teacher's and students' notebooks):

1. God's command and His plan (Deuteronomy 1:1-18).
2. The lessons of disobedience and discipline (Deuteronomy 1:19-2:29).
3. The lessons of obedience and victory (Deuteronomy 2:30-3:22).
4. The lesson learned because of dishonoring God (Deuteronomy 3:23-4:24).

The verse to be memorized:

The LORD thy God, He is God, the faithful God.
(Deuteronomy 7:9a)

THE LESSON

Have you ever been with others on a hiking and camping trip? Where did you go? How long were you gone? Were all the hikers the same age? Who was the leader? (*Teacher:* encourage discussion.) How would you like to take a hiking-camping trip with thousands of parents, children, babies, goats, sheep, and cattle? (See Exodus 12:37-38.) Suppose the trip lasted more than 2,000 weeks (40 years)?

Deuteronomy, the Bible book which we shall be studying in this series, is the record of that kind of journey. Forty years before Deuteronomy opens, the people of Israel had been in Egypt. There they had lived more than 400 years. (See Exodus 12:40-41.) But God had chosen the Israelites for Himself (Deuteronomy 14:2). And He had chosen the land of Canaan as their homeland (Exodus 6:4). To get to Canaan, they would have to hike, camping along the way. Altogether there were about 2,000,000 people to be led by an 80-year-old man of God's choosing–Moses.

After wandering through the wilderness for 40 years, the Israelite people were eager to get settled. Finally they were camped east of the Jordan River (in Moab) with their homeland in sight. But instead of entering at once, they had to wait while Moses (now 120 years old) spent about a month reminding them of many things. Most of the adults had been young when the journey began. So Moses retold the highlights of their trip, telling them especially of the faithfulness of God. Deuteronomy is the record of what he told them.

1. GOD'S COMMAND AND HIS PLAN
Deuteronomy 1:1-18

Show Illustration #1

Standing before the Israelites, Moses began, "The Lord our God spoke to us 40 years ago saying, 'You have lived in Egypt long enough . . . . Take your journey . . . to the land of Canaan . . . . Go in and take possession of the land which the Lord promised to give you.'" (See Deuteronomy 1:6-8; compare Exodus 3:1-8.)

So, right from the beginning, the people had known what God wanted them to do.

Moses reminded the Israelites that God's work was to be done carefully and in an orderly way. "I told you before (at Mount Horeb [Sinai]) that I could not take care of you by myself. I said, 'The Lord God has multiplied you so that you are as the stars of Heaven for multitude . . . . Choose wise and experienced men from your tribes, and I will put them in charge of you.' You agreed this was a good idea. So I took the men you chose and appointed them over you–leaders of thousands, of hundreds, of fifties, and of tens. And at that time I commanded you all the things which you should do."

By knowing God's command in advance and by following His plan, the Israelites soon could have been in their homeland–the land which God, the faithful One, had chosen for them.

2. THE LESSONS OF DISOBEDIENCE AND DISCIPLINE
Deuteronomy 1:19-2:29

Just outside Canaan, Moses reminded the Israelites that 38 years earlier (see Deuteronomy 2:14), two years after leaving Egypt, they had camped at Kadesh Barnea. This was at the southern border of the land the Lord had promised them. There Moses had announced, "Let us move in and take over. The land is ours. God has given it to us." (See Numbers 13:2-14:45.)

But the people had rebelled against God and answered "NO! We shall send in some men to spy out the land." Which is what they did. After 40 days two of the men (Joshua and Caleb) brought an encouraging report. But the other ten spies brought bad news. And the people listened to the ten.

Moses continued, "God said *He* would fight for you. But you did not believe the Lord your God." (See Deuteronomy 1:27-3 3.) What a pity! First the people were guilty of rebelling against God. Second, they were guilty of not believing God. (See Hebrews 3:7-19.)

Moses reminded them that he was not the only one who knew of their rebellion and unbelief. "The Lord God heard you that day and He was angry. Sternly He announced, 'Not one person who is now over the age of 20 (except Joshua and Caleb) will be allowed to go into the land.' "

Then the people had shouted, "We have sinned against the Lord. We will go up and fight as the Lord our God commanded us." They did go but without God's permission or His promise of protection.

"So I spoke to you," Moses reminded them. "But you would not hear. You rebelled against the commandment of the Lord and went presumptuously (going without God's permission)." (See Deuteronomy 1:43.) They had acted boldly and sinfully– presuming God would be with them. But He was not. So the people in the mountains (the Amonites) had come out and chased them like a swarm of bees.

Moses added, "You came down from the mountain crying many tears. But God would not listen to you." The Lord knew their hearts. They weren't sorry for their sins: rebellion, unbelief and presumption. They were crying because they got caught. For their sin, God had disciplined [punished] them severely. He turned them out into the wilderness to wander for 40 years–a year for every day they had spent searching the land. (See Numbers 14:34.)

Show Illustration #2
There in the wilderness all who were more than 20 years old died and were buried–never able to live in the land God had given them.

So Moses was warning the younger generation, "Learn these lessons from the past sins of our people. God is faithful. Obey Him and you will have His blessing. If you disobey Him, you will be disciplined." What a pity that they had not loved Him enough to obey Him willingly!

3. THE LESSONS OF OBEDIENCE AND VICTORY
Deuteronomy 2:30-3:22

Camping there at the edge of the promised land of Canaan, the people must have become impatient. They were eager to see their homeland–a land which was new to all of them. But Moses had more–much more–to say to them. It was as if he said, "Sorry; we cannot move in yet."

Then he reminded them of two more things which had happened in their wilderness years. "Remember King Sihon," Moses continued. "God had commanded us to go through his land, giving us this promise: 'I have given King Sihon and his land into your hand. Take possession and fight against him. This day I will cause people everywhere to be afraid of you.' Sihon would not give us permission to go through his land peacefully. He and all his people fought against us."

Show Illustration #3
Moses added, "But the Lord our God gave King Sihon to us. We defeated him, captured all his cities, and completely destroyed everybody and everything–except the cattle (See Numbers 21:21-32.) Then we turned and went up the road (to Bashan. There King Og and all his people came out to fight against us. But the Lord told me, 'Do not be afraid of him. For I have given him, his people, and all his land to you.' So, as with King Sihon, we completely destroyed everything except the cattle." (See Numbers 21:33-35.)

Being reminded of the defeat of the two kings helped the people of Israel to remember this important lesson: obey God and He will fight for you. (See Deuteronomy 3:21-22; compare John 15:5, 10, 14.)

4. THE LESSON LEARNED BECAUSE OF DISHONORING GOD
Deuteronomy 3:23-4:24

On the border of the Israelites' homeland, Moses reminded them of a hard lesson which he himself had learned. The people had been thirsty but there was no water anywhere. Angrily they blamed Moses. He knew that God is always faithful and that He alone could supply water. So Moses fell on his face and prayed. God answered saying, "Take your rod. Call the leaders together. SPEAK to the rock and water will flow out–plenty for all the people and their animals."

So Moses had gathered the people. "Listen, you rebels!" he exclaimed harshly. "Must we bring water out of this rock?" As everyone watched, he lifted his rod, struck the rock twice, and streams of water gushed out. (Remember! He struck the rock instead of speaking to it.)

Show Illustration #4
Immediately God said to him, "Moses, you have done wrong. You did not believe Me. You are the leader of My people. They follow your example. You disobeyed Me. You did not give glory

to Me, nor did you honor Me before My people. Because of your sin, you will not be allowed to lead My people into the land which I promised them. You will die here." (See Numbers 20:2-13.)

Think of it! After 40 long years of leading those rebellious, stubborn people, God would not let Moses go into the land. Moses told the people he had coaxed the Lord, saying, " 'You have begun to show me Your greatness and Your strong hand . . . . Please let me cross over and see the good land.' But the Lord God was angry with me on your account, and would not listen to me. He commanded, 'Enough! Do not speak to Me again about this. You may go up to the top of the mountain and see the land. But you will not cross over this Jordan River.' "

Moses had been a great leader whom God had trusted. But he was severely punished as an example to us. God will not put up with anger. Nor will He honor or bless those who dishonor Him.

Are you guilty of the sins of the Israelites? Perhaps you have turned against God (rebellion). Or maybe you have not believed His words (unbelief). Or are you doing something which God has not given you permission to do (presumption)? (*Teacher:* give examples or have discussion.) Have you, like Moses, dishonored God? Disobedience of any kind is sin. You may ask God's forgiveness right now. (Encourage silent prayer.)

Now think about the many good things God has done for you. (Maybe some will share their blessings with the others.) Will you thank Him for His goodness and tell God you love Him? Do you love Him enough to obey Him? If so, will you tell Him exactly how you plan to obey Him this week?

Lesson 2
THE COMMANDMENTS REPEATED

NOTE TO THE TEACHER

Deuteronomy is referred to over 80 times in the New Testament. The Lord Christ quoted from it more than any other Old Testament book. So our study is of great importance.

As we saw in our last lesson, the first of Moses' three speeches recorded in Deuteronomy reviews the history of the nation of Israel. Because of their disobedience and unbelief, they were in the wilderness 40 years.

Moses' second sermon is contained in chapters 5 through 26. Because God is faithful, He wanted His people to be in the land He had promised them. Only by their obedience could He lead them to conquer and enjoy the land.

God did not give "suggestions." He gave commands. Almost as soon as the Ten Commandments were given, the Israelites broke the very first one. So in his speech at the edge of Canaan, Moses reminded them that they had turned from God to worship the golden calf. God's stern discipline should have been a constant reminder that He hates disobedience and must punish it. Although the Lord repeatedly warned against this particular sin, the Israelites never learned their lesson. And for that disobedience they paid, and are still paying! It is "a fearful thing to fall into the hands of the living God" (Hebrews 10:31).

God's faithfulness to His own is further proved by His giving them complete details for living in the promised land. He gave them rules for governing their eating, personal cleanliness, and forgiving of debts. God left nothing to chance, for He wanted His people to be happy and able to enjoy His blessings.

The Old Testament laws and related commandments about daily living are similar to the New Testament teachings about Christian living. For example, we are to love the Lord our God with all our heart, soul, and mind. We are to have no other gods. We are to love our neighbors. We are to teach God's Word to others. The wonderful unity of the Word of God is proved by the fact that the same truths appear in both the Old and New Testaments.

Your students may not understand the true story which opens this lesson. In that case, use an appropriate illustration of showing gratitude.

Scripture to be studied: Deuteronomy 4:44-15:18

The *aim* of the lesson: To show that God expects obedience and blesses it.

What your students should *know*: Because God is faithful, He gives us His Word so we can know how to live.

What your students should *feel*: Grateful that God has given us a perfect Guidebook–the Bible.

What your students should *do*: Determine to show love to God by studying His Word and doing loving deeds for others.

Lesson outline (for the teacher's and students' notebooks):

1. Because of His faithfulness, God provided laws for His people (Deuteronomy 4:44-11:32).
2. Because God is faithful, He punishes disobedience (Deuteronomy 9:6-10:20).
3. God's people are to know God's laws and teach them to others (Deuteronomy 5:1-6, 9; 11:18-24).
4. God's law teaches His people to love others (Deuteronomy 15:1-18).

The verse to be memorized:

The LORD thy God, He is God, the faithful God.
(Deuteronomy 7:9a)

THE LESSON

Dick and his parents were trying to find a place to camp overnight. Finally they saw a spot which was exactly right. Finding the farmer who owned the land, they received permission to pitch their tent. Just as they settled down for the night, the wind howled and the tent went flap, flap. Lightning flashed, followed by loud cracks of thunder. Rain beat against the tent and soon it sagged. Dick scrambled to his feet and thrashed about wildly crying, "Dad, Dad! What can we do? The mud is oozing through my toes! The tent is wrapped around my head! How can we get out of here?"

Before his father could answer, a beam of light filled the tent. And a voice boomed above the noisy storm. "Come on! Jump in my truck! You folks will stay with us tonight." And, more quickly than it can be told, Dick and his parents, dripping wet, hopped into the truck with the farmer. In the house, they borrowed some dry clothes. And together with the farmer and his wife, they sang hymns until the storm had passed.

Now Dick is grown and has children of his own. But he still remembers that farmer. What one desire do you suppose Dick has? (*Teacher:* encourage discussion.) He would like to do something nice for the farmer. Why? To show his gratitude for being rescued the night he was terrified.

God had rescued the Israelites–the people He chose for Himself–from their slavery in Egypt. For 40 years He cared for them in the wilderness. He fought battles for them. He kept their shoes and clothes from wearing out (Deuteronomy 29:5). He gave them water and food. He showed them mercy when they sinned. Why? Because they were a big, important nation? No! (See Deuteronomy 7:6-8.) Because they were good? No! (See Deuteronomy 9:5-6.) God was faithful to the people of Israel because He loved them.

Camped at the edge of the land God had promised to give them, the people listened to three speeches which Moses made. Throughout the first one (which we studied in our last lesson), Moses reminded them of God's faithfulness in the wilderness. As a result of His faithfulness, what could the Lord expect from the Israelites? (Encourage student response.) Moses said, "Fear the Lord your God, walk in all His ways, love Him, and serve Him with all your heart and all your soul." (See Deuteronomy 10:12.)

1. BECAUSE OF HIS FAITHFULNESS, GOD PROVIDED LAWS FOR HIS PEOPLE
Deuteronomy 4:44-11:32

God's people were to fear Him and walk in all His ways. They knew God loved them. They had enjoyed His faithfulness. But Moses reminded them (in his second speech), that they were to fear the Lord. For those who had been too young to remember, he explained what had happened when God gave His laws 40 years before. (See Deuteronomy 4:11-12.)

Show Illustration #5

Thunder rolled! Lightning flashed! A trumpet sounded! Moses had brought the trembling people out of the camp to meet with God. Smoke rose from the mountain! Fire blazed! The whole mountain shook! The trumpet sounded louder! And God called Moses to the top of the mountain.

Moses returned shortly with a strict warning: "Do not break through the boundaries trying to see God. If you do, you will die!" The Israelites, shivering with fear, moved farther from the mountain.

Moses continued, "God is waiting for me at the mountaintop. I must return now. Stay away from the mountain!"

"Yes, yes!" the people had chorused. "God has shown us His glory and His greatness. We have heard His voice out of the fire. We have seen that God talks with man . . . . If we hear the voice of the Lord our God any more, we shall die . . . . You go, Moses, and hear everything the Lord our God says. Then you can tell us and we shall hear and do it." (See Deuteronomy 5:24-27.)

God had given Moses many commands and rules on the mountaintop. The rules told the people how to worship God and how to act toward others. There were ten commandments, beginning with, "You must not worship any other god but Me. You must not make or worship any idol." Another said, "You must not murder." Then, "You must not steal." And, "You must not lie." Finally, "You must not want what belongs to someone else."

There was much, much more. At last Moses had come down from the mountain. He told the people what God had commanded. When they heard the laws and rules, the Israelites again promised, "All the words which the Lord has said, we shall do and be obedient." (See Exodus 24:3, 7.)

How faithful, how loving God was to give them commands and rules! Now His people knew exactly what He wanted them to do. They understood they would have His blessing IF they obeyed His laws.

2. BECAUSE GOD IS FAITHFUL, HE PUNISHES DISOBEDIENCE
Deuteronomy 9:6-10:20

God had again called, "Moses, come up to Me on the mountaintop. I have written My commands on tablets of stone. You can teach them to My people." (See Exodus 31:18.)

Because Moses was gone many days, God's people (the Israelites) had become restless. To Aaron (Moses' brother) they said, "Moses, our leader, has disappeared. Something must have happened to him. Make us a god to lead us."

Imagine that! The first two commands God had given were (1) "You must not make or worship any other god but Me," and (2) "You must not make or worship any idol." The Israelites had agreed to obey all the laws and commands. Now, with their own lips, they asked for another god–an idol, a false nothing.

"Give me your golden earrings," Aaron had demanded. From them he made a golden calf. And the people whom God had chosen for His special treasure, turned from Him to the calf god.

When Moses came down from the mountain, carrying the Ten Commandments which God Himself had written on stone. He saw the people dancing before the calf. Moses angrily smashed the tablets to the ground. "You have turned your backs on the living and powerful One," he shouted. "You have chosen to worship an idol. God will not allow this!"

Show Illustration #6

That night, 3,000 men lay dead, slain by the Levites, as God had commanded. Why? Those 3,000 had led the others away from the true and living God to an idol. (See Exodus 32:1-28.)

At the edge of Canaan Moses repeatedly reminded the people of the seriousness of having other gods. (See Deuteronomy 6:14-15; 7:4, 16, 25; 8:19-20; 11:16-17; 12:2-3, 30-32; 13:6-11, 13-16.) The Israelites had much to think about. Would they always remember that God had given them His laws for their good? Would they obey God because of His goodness to them?

3. GOD'S PEOPLE ARE TO KNOW GOD'S LAWS AND TEACH THEM TO OTHERS
Deuteronomy 5:1-6:9; 11:18-24

Again God (through Moses) repeated the Ten Commandments to His people. (*Teacher:* review these, using Old Testament Volume 9 of this series, showing illustrations 2-4.)

These commands (and about 600 others!) were holy and good. To receive God's blessing, the people had to obey all the laws. To disobey a command was sin, (See Deuteronomy 27:26.) and sin had to be punished.

Show Illustration #7

Fathers and mothers listened carefully as Moses announced, "These words, which I command you this day, shall be in your heart. You must teach them diligently to your children . . . . Talk of them when you sit in your house and when you walk outside, and when you lie down, and when you get up. Write them upon the posts of your house, and on your gates." (See Deuteronomy 6:6-9; 11:18-24.)

This was God's way. Fathers were to learn God's laws and teach them to their children. The children, when they were grown, would teach their children. God never changes. He still expects fathers to teach His Word to their children. (See Ephesians 6:4.)

4. GOD'S LAW TEACHES HIS PEOPLE TO LOVE OTHERS
Deuteronomy 15:1-18

God also commanded, "You are to love the Lord your God with all your heart, with all your soul, and with all your might" (Deuteronomy 6:5). If His people would obey this one command, it would help them to obey all the others.

Show Illustration #8

For example, if they loved God perfectly, it would not be hard to obey this rule: "When you see someone who is poor and needs help, do something about it. Fill your hands with things to give him and give to him cheerfully. For this, the Lord your God will bless you in all your works, and in all that you put your hand to." (See Deuteronomy 15:7-11.) God would be pleased when His people obeyed Him. But He would also bless them for their obedience.

Lesson 3
TWO CHOICES FOR GOD'S PEOPLE

NOTE TO THE TEACHER

In this section of the Book of Deuteronomy, Moses sets before the Israelites two ways: (1) the way of blessing and (2) the way of cursing. In simple language (Deuteronomy 30:11, 14) he reminds the people that they have two choices in their relationship with God–to obey or disobey. These choices are so important that the word "life" is used as a result of choosing to obey. The word "death" is used as a result of choosing to disobey.

There is only one right way–God's way. God's way (recorded in the Word of God) teaches us everything we need to know to follow His will. Because of His faithfulness, those who obediently choose His way will receive His blessing.

God does not force people to obey Him. He is not pleased with those who obey only to avoid punishment. In Moses' day the Lord wanted people who, because of their love for Him, gave themselves willingly. He wants the same kind of person today. One who truly loves God and is grateful to Him will make the right choice–obedience.

Canaan, the land God had chosen for His treasured people, was a land of idols. For this reason, He commanded the Israelite people to destroy the Canaanites and others who lived there. God wanted His own for Himself. He did not want them to be ignorant of His laws and commands. So He had Moses review them beforehand while the Israelites camped at the Jordan River. Later, when they would enter the land, they were to erect stones on which parts of the law were to be copied. The Israelites would then have a lasting record of what God wanted them to do. If they disobeyed, they would have no excuse. Because the Lord is faithful, His promised blessings for obedience should have encouraged them to live to please Him. But they failed. What a pity!

Teacher, does your life please God? Are you serving Him gladly because you love Him? (See 1 Peter 5:2-4.) Do others see in you a life of obedience to the Word of God? You must choose God's way if you would successfully lead others in His way.

Scripture to be studied: Deuteronomy 11:26-28; 16:1–30:20

The *aim* of the lesson: To show that God promises blessing for obedience and discipline for disobedience.

What your students should *know*: Everyone has two choices: (1) to obey God or (2) to disobey Him.

What your students should *feel*: A desire to please God by living a life of obedience to Him.

What your students should *do*:
Unsaved: Choose God's way of salvation.
Saved: Determine to obey God in the choices they must make today.

Lesson outline (for the teacher's and students' notebooks):
1. God warns of discipline for disobedience (Deuteronomy 27:14-26; 28:15-19).
2. The blessings for obedience (Deuteronomy 28:1-14).
3. The results of disobedience (Deuteronomy 28:20-68; 29:16-29).
4. The greatest of all blessings (Deuteronomy 18:15-19).

The verse to be memorized:
The LORD thy God, He is God, the faithful God.
(Deuteronomy 7:9a)

THE LESSON

"Please, Mother, may we visit Aunt Betty on Saturday?" Susan begged. "There's going to be a wonderful feast (or celebration). I know she wants us to come."

"Well, we can go if we all help to get the work done," her mother answered.

"What can I do?" Susan asked quickly.

"Take some baskets and pick up all the apples that have fallen off the tree," her mother instructed. (*Teacher:* Name fruit familiar to your students.) "You'll have to be careful, because the bees like the fallen apples. Put the good apples in one basket, and those which are completely bad into another one."

How much the children of Israel had to learn and remember! But everything God told them, every law He gave them, was for their good. And He gave them these rules because He loved His people. All He wanted was their love in return. And He wants

"But, Mother, rotten apples are so squooshy," Susan protested. your love, too.

Do you love the Lord God? Do you love His Word? Do you study it each day? Do you teach His Word to others? Are you busy doing deeds of love for others? We are born into God's family only through faith in the Lord Jesus Christ. But loving acts should follow.

I am going to ask these questions again. Answer to God silently after each one. If you must answer *no* to any of them, will you tell God that you want to be able to answer *yes* from this day on? Ask Him to forgive you for failing before. Tell Him exactly how you plan to correct your failures. Thank Him for being willing to help you. (*Teacher:* repeat questions in preceding paragraph.)

Now will you write in your notebook what you believe God wants you to do? Add exactly how you plan to accomplish His will.

"I know," Mother admitted. "But do it for me anyway. And do it cheerfully. If you do, you will go to Aunt Betty's house. If not, there will be no trip."

Now, what was the next step for Susan to take? What choices did she have? (Encourage response.) Susan could choose to obey and get the reward. Or she could disobey, and miss out on the treat. But she had to make the choice.

Susan really wanted that trip to Aunt Betty's. And she also wanted to please her mother whom she loved. So she chose to obey. Immediately she went outside, got the baskets and gathered the apples, humming as she did.

Almost every day you, too, have choices to make. You can make the right choice or the wrong choice. You may choose your own way or God's way.

1. GOD WARNS OF DISCIPLINE FOR DISOBEDIENCE
Deuteronomy 27:14-26; 28:15-19

Long ago, the people of Israel learned the importance of making choices. While they were camped near the Jordan River just before entering the land of Canaan, God (through Moses) gave them instructions.

"When you cross the river into Canaan, your homeland," Moses began, "set up large, smooth stones. Plaster them and plainly write God's laws on them. Using rough stones, build an altar to the Lord. On it, offer burnt offerings to God, showing that you are giving yourselves completely to Him. Offer peace offerings with praise to show that you choose to obey Him."

Show Illustration #9

Then Moses said, "When you get into Canaan, six of the 12 tribes should stand on Mount Gerizim. The other tribes are to stand on Mount Ebal. All of God's commands will be read to you loudly that day," Moses declared. "You will be reminded of God's discipline for disobeying His laws, and you will hear of His blessings for obedience. As each command is read, you are to answer, 'Amen' (meaning, Let it be as God has said)."

So that all of God's commands would be understood, Moses reviewed them one by one:

"You will be under a curse and out of favor with God if you make any kind of image, hide it away and worship it." God wanted His people to remember that nothing can be kept secret from Him. He can see even hidden idols. And He knew that when His people got into Canaan, instead of worshiping Him alone, they would be tempted to worship idols.

Moses continued, "God also commands: 'Anyone who dishonors his mother or father shall be under a curse.....Anyone who sins against a neighbor, a stranger, a family member–or anyone else–by cheating them or harming their bodies, will be under a curse.'" Moses read one command after another.

2. THE BLESSINGS FOR OBEDIENCE
Deuteronomy 28:1-14

God did not want His people to be cursed. Indeed, He, the faithful One, promised, "If you will obey Me, I will make you the head of all the nations. You will be the most important–not the tail. Everything you do will go right."

Show Illustration #10

God added, "If you obey My commands, you will have fine crops and cattle. Your families will be healthy. You will not have to borrow money. Other nations will wish to be like you. They will be afraid to fight you because I, the Lord, will be on your side. You will be able to enjoy the wonderful land peacefully."

The Lord God continued, "I have set before you blessing and cursing."

Because God is faithful, He was ready and willing to bless His people if they would love and obey Him. They were free to choose what they would do. However, they were not free to choose the consequences.

3. THE RESULTS OF DISOBEDIENCE
Deuteronomy 28:20-68; 29:16-29

Exactly what curses would come upon the people of Israel if they chose to disobey God? Moses made it perfectly clear, explaining, "Nothing will go right for you. You will have terrible trouble. Your crops will not grow. You will have dreadful sicknesses. Your cattle, your sons, your daughters will be stolen from you. Some will be punished with blindness. Others will go insane. Some will be killed and eaten by birds."

Show Illustration #11

Through Moses, God told that there would be other results for disobedience. "You, My people, will be forced out of the land I have given you. You will be taken as prisoners by enemies. Instead of staying together as a strong nation, you will be scattered from one end of the earth to the other. You will be like the tail of an animal–the least important nation. People will mock you and hiss at you. All nations will ask, 'Why has the Lord done this? Why is He so angry?' Then men will answer, 'Because they have disobeyed the Lord God. They served other gods and worshiped them . . . . And the Lord rooted them out of their land in anger.'"

How faithfully God warned His people! The very thought of disobedience should have terrified them. Instead, time after time they chose their own way instead of God's.

True to His word, God caused them to be taken as captives into other lands. And today, more than 3,000 years later, most of the Israelite people are scattered from one end of the earth to the other. They still do not have all the land which God had promised them. What a price to pay for disobedience! Yet God loves them. He chose them long ago as a treasure for Himself.

4. THE GREATEST OF ALL BLESSINGS
Deuteronomy 18:15-19

God promised the Israelites many good things. But the best of all His blessings they refused to receive. On the edge of Canaan, God promised them (through Moses): "The Lord God will raise up for you a Prophet from among your own countrymen . . . . I, the Lord, will put My words in His mouth. And He will speak all that I command Him . . . . But I shall hold responsible whoever refuses to listen to My words which He will speak." (See Deuternomy 18:15-19.)

Did the people at that time understand who the promised Prophet would be? We are not told. However, some 1400 years later the Israelites were looking for the coming of God's Prophet. (See John 1:19-21; 6:14; 7:40.)

Show Illustration #12

The Lord Jesus Christ plainly pro-phesied, "I shall be killed and after three days rise again" (Mark 8:31). And "Destroy this temple [My body] and in three days I shall raise it up" (John 2:18-22). Here was God's Prophet, speaking God's words. And what He foretold came true. The people did kill Him. In His death, He offered Himself as the perfect sacrifice for the sins of the world. (See John 10:15-18; Hebrews 9:26-28; 10:12.) The third day He rose from the dead, proving He is indeed the promised One: the Saviour, God the Son. But the nation of Israel would not receive Him. (See John 1:12.) By refusing Him, they would not have eternal life. Neither can you.

Today you must make a choice. If you have never placed your trust in the Lord Jesus Christ, you do not have eternal life. (See John 3:15-16; 6:47; 10:28; 17:2-3.) You will be separated from God forever. However, you can choose to turn to Him and receive him as your Saviour from sin. To choose Christ is to receive everlasting life and to be certain of being with Him in Heaven forever. Will you turn to Him now, this moment?

If you are already a child of God through faith in Christ, you have to make decisions every day. Right now you may be trying to choose between something God wants you to do or doing what you want to do. Even if God's way may be hard or unpopular, will you choose what He wants you to do? (*Teacher:* students may want to tell what choices they face and ask for the prayers of their classmates.)

Will you list in your notebook the choices you have to make today, this week? Write down exactly what you must do in order to choose God's way. Remember: because He is faithful, He is ready to bless you when you obey Him.

Lesson 4
MOSES PREPARES TO LEAVE THIS WORLD

NOTE TO THE TEACHER

Moses was a great man in many ways: a great lawgiver, prophet, teacher, and leader. He was intelligent, well-taught, brave, and strong. Best of all, he was a man who trusted in the living, faithful God of Heaven. His love for the Lord made him obedient (with one exception–see lesson 1, section 40. He was content to serve according to God's directions.

God had a purpose for saving Moses' life when he was a baby. The Lord needed a human leader to do something extremely important. He chose Moses for the task, training and preparing him for 80 years. Then Moses led the Israelites for 40 years. Moses understood the faithfulness of God and His plan for His people. With all his energies, Moses pled with the Israelites to give hearty, loving obedience to the Lord.

God revealed through Moses the future He has planned for His people. Moses was eager for the people to be obedient so they could enjoy the amazing glories God wanted to give them. He warned them against disobedience and its dreadful consequences. Then–at age 120–his work was finished. In his farewell messages he reminded the people four times that he could not enter the Promised Land. Even today, some 3,400 years later, his one act of disobedience continues to be an object lesson. He had to suffer the results of his sin.

Unselfishly Moses begged the people to go in and possess the land, fearlessly following their new leader, Joshua. Joshua would reap what Moses had sown. That did not make the work of Moses any less important. God rewards faithfulness, not results only. So take heart, teacher. You may be sowing the Word of God today in some lives which seemingly are not affected. But in the future there may be a real spiritual harvest in those lives. Even if you are not the one who is allowed to see the results, remember: God–who is absolutely faithful– rewards the faithfulness of His own. (See 1 Corinthians 4:2.)

Scripture to be studied: Deuteronomy 3:23-28; 4:21-24; 31:1–34:12

The *aim* of the lesson: To show that as God faithfully cared for Moses and the children of Israel, so He will care for those whose trust is in the Saviour.

What your students should *know*: Because God is absolutely faithful, He can be trusted always.

What your students should *feel*: Gratitude for God's great faithfulness.

What your students should *do*: Determine exactly how they plan to obey God today and this week.

Lesson outline (for the teacher's and students' notebooks):

1. Moses commands the people to take possession of the land (Deuteronomy 31:1-13).

2. Moses writes a song to be sung (Deuteronomy 31:14-32:52).
3. Moses gives his last message (Deuteronomy 33).
4. Moses' work is finished (Deuteronomy 34).

The verse to be memorized:

The LORD thy God, He is God, the faithful God.
(Deuteronomy 7:9a)

THE LESSON

Think what it would be like to be part of a small wandering nation which knows almost nothing about war. Suppose you had to face and fight seven strong, fierce nations living in well-protected, walled cities. (See Deuteronomy 7:1.) And you are reminded that your splendid leader will not be allowed to go with you. Does this sound frightening? How would you feel?

1. MOSES COMMANDS THE PEOPLE TO TAKE POSSESSION OF THE LAND
Deuteronomy 31:1-13

This is exactly the problem the Israelites had. For 40 years they had been led by Moses through the wilderness. Finally they were camped on the border of the land God had promised them. Then Moses announced, "I am now 120 years old. The Lord has told me I cannot go over the Jordan River with you. But the Lord God will go over before you. He will destroy these nations . . . and you will own the land . . . . Be strong and of good courage. Do not be afraid of the people. For the Lord your God will go with you. He will not fail you nor forsake you."

Show Illustration #13

Then Moses called Joshua whom the people knew well. (See Numbers 27:15-23.) Before all the Israelites Moses gave orders to Joshua:

"Be strong! Have courage! For you must go with these people into the land which the Lord has promised to give them . . . . And the Lord will go before you. He will be with you.

He will not fail you nor forsake you. Fear not! Do not be afraid!"

With such a big responsibility, Joshua surely needed these words of encouragement.

Moses had something else to do. He wrote down God's laws and commands. He then gave them to the priests and leaders. "Keep this Book of the Law in a safe place," he ordered. "At the end of every seven years, the people will gather [during the feast of tabernacles] to worship the Lord. At that time, always read all these words to everyone: men, women, children, and visiting strangers. They must all hear and learn His Word so they will fear God. Be careful to obey all His laws."

The Lord is always interested in and concerned about children. So He caused Moses to add: "And teach God's Word to all the children who will be born." (See Deuteronomy 31:13.)

2. MOSES WRITES A SONG TO BE SUNG
Deuteronomy 31:14–32:52

The Lord then told Moses, "Call Joshua. I want to meet you and him at the tabernacle." There the Lord said, "Moses, you are about to die. After you are gone, My people will turn from Me and worship false gods. They will break the agreement [covenant] which I made with them. Then I shall be angry with them," God declared. "I shall turn from them. And they will have dreadful troubles."

God added, "I am going to give you a song to teach the people. The song will remind them of Me. And it will help them to remember that I warned them of punishment if they turned from Me." (See Deuteronomy 31:19, 21.)

Show Illustration #14

So that same day, Moses wrote the song God gave him. It began:

Listen, O heavens; hear,
O earth, these words . . .
Our God is great . . . .
He is the Rock!
His work is perfect and
all He does is right
God cared for His people
and guarded them . . . .
The Lord guided His people and provided for them.
But you, the people of God, have sacrificed to strange gods.
You neglected the Rock and forgot
the God who formed you . . . .
Therefore you, My people–young and old–
will be destroyed with the sword.
You will be filled with terror . . . .
You will be scattered . . . .
I, the Lord, shall judge My people . . .
But I shall show mercy.

(*Teacher:* you may use more of the song, depending upon the ability of your students. We have included only a few thoughts taken from Deuteronomy 32:1, 3-4, 10, 12-14, 17-18, 25-26, 36, 43.)

Every time the people sang the song, they would be reminded of God's faithfulness. They would also remember their own disobedience. And they couldn't forget that any punishment which came from God was exactly as He had warned.

Moses added this promise: "Obey all the words of God's law and you shall live long in your homeland." (See Deuteronomy 32:46-47.)

Right after receiving the song and teaching it to the people, Moses had orders from God. "Climb to the top of the mountain. From there you will see the land of Canaan. I have given that land to My people, the Israelites. But you will die on the mountain because you sinned against Me. You did not honor Me before My people. So though you will see the land, you will not go into it."

Poor Moses! He had done many good things. He had been a fine leader. But because of his being a leader, God had to judge him more severely when he sinned. Do you remember what sin he committed? (*Teacher:* Review Numbers 20:7-13. See Old Testament, Volume 14, lesson 2 of this series.)

3. MOSES GIVES HIS LAST MESSAGE
Deuteronomy 33

Moses turned to give his last message to the people. He reminded them of the time God had come to Mount Sinai in a thick cloud with lightning. There He had given His law to His people because, Moses said, "God loves you." (See Deuteronomy 33:3.) Naming the heads of the tribes one by one, Moses spoke words of blessing.

Once again he reminded the Israelites of the Lord's faithfulness: "The eternal God is your refuge, and underneath are the everlasting arms." (See Deuteronomy 33:27; Romans 8:31.)

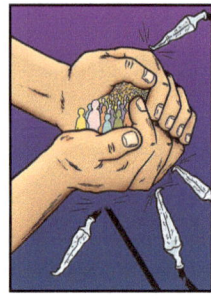

Show Illustration #15

What comforting words for the fearful people at the edge of the land of Canaan! They were to have possession of that land, but only after they met and fought the seven strong nations which lived there. They would have to do this without their experienced leader, Moses. As a kind and loving father, he reminded them that God, the eternal One, would protect them. He would hold them in His everlasting arms.

Moses added, "God will chase out the enemy before you. Destroy that enemy and you will live safely in the land. There you will have plenty to eat and drink. O Israel, you are a people saved by the Lord. He, your Shield, is the One who helps you. Your enemies will cringe before you." (See Deuteronomy 33:28-29.)

What wonderful promises God gave His people! When they arrived in their new homeland, would they remember His warnings? Would they destroy the idols–the false, make-believe gods–in Canaan? Would they, the people of God, live pure lives, seeking to please Him always? Would they trust the strong, faithful, eternal One?

4. MOSES' WORK IS FINISHED
Deuteronomy 34

Moses turned from the people he loved. Thoughtfully he climbed the mountain, as God had commanded him. Though he was 120 years old, he was still strong. He could see clearly. Up, up, up he went–alone. What were the people thinking as they watched their leader disappear from sight? Were they sorry for the unkind things they had said about him and to him? Did they feel bad because they were the ones who had caused him to be impatient–impatient enough to disobey God? Do you think they prayed for Moses?

(*Teacher:* if you wish, show Illustration #16 from Old Testament Volume 14 of this series.)

What a wonderful time Moses had on that mountain, alone with God, hearing the Lord talk to him! God allowed Moses a glorious view of the land of promise. He saw, far below, the Dead Sea, the winding Jordan River, the fertile green valleys. He could see the city of Jericho with its waving palm trees, the Sea of Galilee, the hills of Bethlehem. God told Moses, "This is the land I promised to Abraham, Isaac, and Jacob. I have caused you to see it with your eyes. But you will not go over there."

"So Moses, the servant of the Lord died [on the mountaintop] . . . according to the word of the Lord" (Deuteronomy 34:5). And God buried him. Where he is buried is God's secret.

Show Illustration #16

Were the people of Israel sad? The Bible says they cried for 30 days mourning for Moses.

At last the time came for the Israelites to cross the Jordan River and take possession of their homeland. Joshua was their new leader. He loved and trusted God as Moses had. God had commanded him not to be afraid. By experience, he knew that God is faithful. So he could trust God perfectly for all the days ahead.

Are you like Joshua? What experiences have you had that prove the faithfulness of God? (*Teacher:* encourage discussion.)

Has God asked you to do something which seems hard, even impossible? Will you promise to do that hard thing today . . . this week? Write in your notebook whatever you believe God has asked you to do. Enter also the steps you will have to take in order to obey the Lord.

If you are afraid to do His will, will you confess your fears to Him? Will you ask Him to make you strong and courageous? Can you say in the words of our memory verse that the Lord your God, "He is God, the faithful God"?

Or are you one who does not know the living and true God of Heaven? You cannot be strong and courageous until you have placed all your trust in His Son, the Lord Jesus Christ. If you have never turned to Him, will you do so right now?

www.ingramcontent.com/pod-product-compliance
Lightning Source LLC
Chambersburg PA
CBHW060805090426
42736CB00002B/170